pocket
cornwall

Exploring the Camel Estuary

Michael Kent
photography Adrian Langdon

Alison Hodge

First published in 2007 by Alison Hodge, Bosulval, Newmill, Penzance, Cornwall TR20 8XA, UK info@alison-hodge.co.uk www.alison-hodge.co.uk

Reprinted 2008

ISBN-13 978-0-906720-52-3

British Library Cataloguing-in-Publication Data
A catalogue record for this book is available from the British Library.

Designed and originated by BDP – Book Design and Production, Penzance, Cornwall

Printed in China

Acknowledgements

Our special thanks go to Merryn Kent for reading through the text, and for her suggestions. We would also like to thank Glynn Bennalick for designing and drawing the map of the Crooked Estuary, and the following for their help: Dom Boothroyd, Manager of Padstow Lobster Hatchery; James Burke, Freshwater Biodiversity Officer, Environment Agency; Anna David, Polzeath Voluntary Marine Wildlife Area; Charlie David, North Cornwall District Council; Ed Derriman, Chief Fishery Officer at the Cornwall Sea Fisheries Committee; Jon Evans, Secretary of the Camel Fisheries Association; Nick Harrison-White, Cornwall Wildlife Trust; Derek Julian, bird recorder for Cornwall Bird Watching and Preservation Society; Derek Lord, National Trust Warden at Pentire; Mike Lawson, former warden of the Camel Trail; Tim Marshall, shell-fisherman and farmer; Captain Trevor Platt, Padstow's Harbour Master; Susie Ray, artist and designer; Richard Smith, Nikki Smith and Matt Slater, Blue Reef Aquarium; Jenni Thomson, Gaia Trust; Stella Turk MBE, Cornwall Wildlife Trust.

Note: All photographs are © Adrian Langdon, except for the following which are © Michael Kent: pages 23, 63 (top left, top right, bottom left); 64 (left, right); 70 (top right); 72 (top).

Contents

Introduction

Rainbow over Trewornan reed-bed

Adrian and I live on the same hill overlooking the Camel Estuary, an area famous for its outstanding natural beauty. Every day we have the privilege of experiencing its splendours and ever-changing moods. Living at Wadebridge has made it easy for us to explore all the main places of interest in and around the estuary at different times of the year.

The River Camel winds its way from its source high on Bodmin Moor down to Padstow and Polzeath and into the Celtic Sea – a journey of about 30 miles. At Polbrock, where freshwater meets seawater brought in by high tides, the river becomes an estuary. The Camel Estuary extends down to Newland and Gulland Rock at its mouth – about six miles as the cormorant flies.

Averaging under half a mile wide, it is not a large estuary, but it is nevertheless magnificent. Within its small confines, the Camel has many habitats. This diversity provides a wealth of scenery that not only varies with location, but also changes dramatically with the state of tide and seasons.

During the largest spring tides more than 30 million cubic metres of seawater move in and out of the estuary. In the course of a year, millions of tonnes of sediment are transferred from one place to another, causing channels to shift by up to 30 metres. This makes the Camel Estuary extraordinarily dynamic and variable, a source of delight to ramblers and naturalists, and an inspiration to artists and poets.

In the following pages we explore the Camel Estuary from the wood-lined banks at its tidal limits to the open waters and exposed shores at its mouth. We will encounter various estuarine habitats, find out about the diverse communities of animals and plants they support, and meet some of the people whose lives affect and are affected by the wildlife of the estuary. Our aim is to share with you the joy of discovering new insights about life in this outstandingly beautiful area.

Michael Kent and Adrian Langdon
Wadebridge, 2007

A note on names

Many organisms mentioned in this book have more than one common name, some have none. Common names may refer to more than one type of animal or plant in different parts of the world – or even in different parts of the county! We therefore give the scientific name of an organism along with its common name when we first make a significant reference to it. The scientific name is double-barrelled and unique; it is the name by which an organism is known throughout the world.

By convention, the full scientific name is written in italics. The first name, always starting with a capital letter, denotes the genus and the second, always starting with a small letter, is the specific name. For example, the scientific name for shags is *Phalacrocorax aristotelis*; the species is *aristotelis* and the genus *Phalacrocorax*. In the same genus are closely related species, such as the cormorant, *Phalacrocorax carbo*, and others.

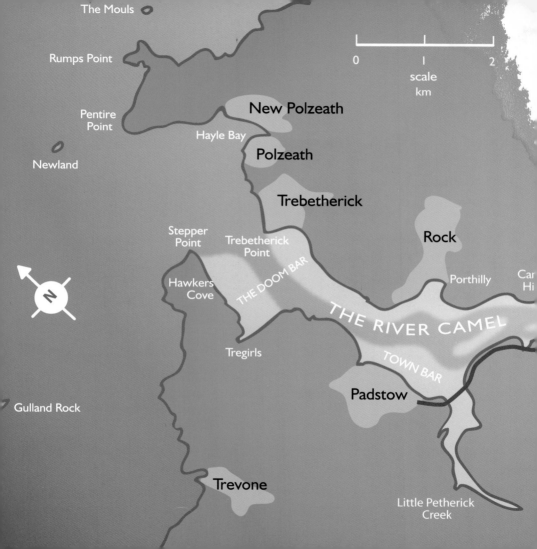

The 'Crooked Estuary'

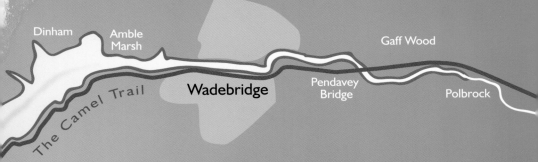

Dinham   Amble Marsh   Gaff Wood

The Camel Trail   Wadebridge   Pendavey Bridge   Polbrock

Slate Quarry

Pinkson Creek

According to some authorities, the word Camel is derived from two Cornish words: Cam meaning crooked, and Hayle, meaning estuary. Even a cursory look at a map of the estuary shows how appropriate this name is.

The Camel Estuary is easily accessible. You can reach all the places mentioned in this book either from the Camel Trail or from public footpaths. If you wish to explore the Camel Estuary following the same route as in this book, start at Polbrock Bridge. From there, explore Gaff Wood. After exiting the wood, follow the Camel Trail all the way to Padstow. From Padstow, take the ferry to Rock to explore the eastern edge of the estuary from Porthilly to Pentire Head. From Pentire, take a look at the Rumps. The Rumps is outside the estuary, but the birds that breed there can regularly be seen feeding on the Camel.

After your excursion to the Rumps, make your way back to Padstow, and then continue along the western side of the estuary, finishing at Stepper Point.

Polbrock to Wadebridge

Polbrock Bridge marks the upper limit of the Camel Estuary. It is where freshwater and seawater meet. Above the Bridge, river water is rarely tainted by sea salts, even on high spring tides. Below the Bridge, the estuary becomes increasingly salty towards Stepper and Pentire.

Few animals can cope with dramatic changes in water saltiness. One that seems to revel in them is the salmon (*Salmo salar*). Look down from Polbrock Bridge into the river, and you might be lucky enough to see an adult resting in a deep pool before it continues its exhausting journey up into the freshwater streams where it breeds. Or you might be surprised by a splash of silver as a young salmon leaps out of the water on its seaward journey.

A salmon breeds and spends its early life in fresh water. Most adults expend so much energy in breeding that they die of exhaustion soon afterwards. Apart from a small yolk sac, the young fish are then left to fend for themselves.

An angler on the Camel near Polbrock

When a Camel salmon is about two years old, it makes its way down the estuary, into the sea and then far up into the cold waters of the North Atlantic. It may travel several hundred miles to reach waters rich in squid and the shrimp-like organisms on which it feeds. After fattening itself on the fruits of the sea for a year or two, it makes its long return journey down the Irish Sea and then up the North Cornwall coast until it tastes the waters of the Camel. It then turns right to make the final stage of its migration up the estuary and back to its breeding site.

It is during this final stage of its journey that fishermen armed with rod, line and bait pit their wits and skill against those of the fish. Usually the fish wins. On the odd occasion that a fisherman lands a catch, few end up in the fridge or cooking pot. Most are returned to finish their epic journey.

The Camel is one of the few estuaries in the South West where salmon are thriving. In many places habitat loss, poor river management, over-fishing and pollution have brought populations to the brink of extinction. Only the cleanest, best-oxygenated

Polbrock Bridge – the upper limit of the Camel Estuary (top). A line-caught salmon (above)

fresh water, rich in wildlife is good enough. This makes the salmon an exceptionally good indicator of high water quality. As long as the salmon thrives in the Camel, we know that all is well.

The success of salmon in the Camel is due partly to the anglers who appear so intent on interrupting their long migration upstream. Jon Evans, the Secretary of the Camel Fisheries Association, told me that the key to maintaining the health of the Camel is to 'look after

the uplands'. The moors are the source of most of the Camel's water. If the tall grasses and mosses are protected and encouraged to grow, the vegetation will soak up water like a sponge. This delays runoff after heavy rains, and reduces the risk of flash floods.

Jon lives at Polbrock, an ideal situation for keeping an eye on the river. The anglers work with other groups, including the Environment Agency, Natural England, local councils, farmers and landowners to conserve the Camel,

An otter on land (top), and in water (above)

Otter spraint (left) and footprints (above)

they spend so much time on the riverbanks. Many have volunteered to become one of Kate Stokes' 'Otter spotters'. Kate is Water for Wildlife Manager and Otter Officer for Cornwall Wildlife Trust. Reported sightings help her to find out how many otters live on the Camel, where they are, and what they are doing at different times of the day and in different seasons. This information is vital for the successful conservation of the otters. (If you would like to become one of Kate's Otter Spotters, or if you want to report an otter sighting, phone 01872 273939, or go to www.cornwallwildlifetrust.org.uk.)

It was on the Camel that Kate first caught sight of Cornish otters. Leaving a Wadebridge hostelry late one evening, she heard what she thought was the characteristic short, shrill cry of a female otter. In eager anticipation,

not only as an excellent salmon river, but also as a wonderful haven for other wildlife, such as otters.

Otters (*Lutra lutra*) roam freely on the Camel from upland pools to estuarine creeks. Footprints and spraints (droppings) are common signs of their presence, but otters are shy and rarely seen in the wild. Anglers are more likely than most to see them because

...e raced down to the old bridge, leaned over the side and was rewarded with a fine display of a female and her cubs frolicking on the foreshore. She stayed there for about 50 minutes in otter-spotter heaven, soaking up the scene conveniently lit by the lamps along the bridge.

Kate's Spotters are already challenging some of our assumptions about otters. Generally regarded as nocturnal animals, some sightings suggest that they are more active during the day than was previously thought. Perhaps the ban on hunting has resulted in a change of behaviour, with the otter feeling it's now safe to venture out in daylight.

Camel anglers also collect spraints for Kate and other experts to analyse. This is not the most glamorous task in wildlife conservation, but it can be very informative. Teasing the spraint apart reveals what the otter has been eating. And DNA analysis of the soft, less savoury sections can tell researchers a lot about the otter's identity.

The Camel has been designated a SAC (Special Area of Conservation) mainly because it is the otter's major stronghold in the South West. The population remained even when those in other areas were decimated by competition with mink and poisoning by pollution. Camel otters have been used to recolonize other parts of England.

The Camel is glorious otter country. Its river and tributaries provide an adequate food supply throughout the year, and its wooded lower reaches give excellent cover for resting and breeding. Its high conservation status will help the Camel to remain a desirable residence for future generations.

Another reason for the Camel being designated a SAC is that it marks the extreme south-west of the range of an important if unassuming little fresh-water fish, the bullhead (*Cottus gobio*). As bullheads generally lie well camouflaged on the riverbed, waiting for unsuspecting prey to come within striking distance, you are unlikely to notice the fish under water. However, because they form an important part of the diet of the kingfisher, there is a good chance of seeing a bullhead in this bird's beak. When attacked, the fish expands its spiny pectoral fins and assumes a dragon-like defensive posture. Before a kingfisher can swallow the fish, it has to beat it against a branch or wall.

Catching sight of a kingfisher (*Alcedo atthis*) is one of the great joys of walking between Polbrock and Wadebridge. Whether streaking in and out of its nesting hole in a riverbank, or diving from a branch overhanging

Kingfisher with bullhead prey

the river, this bird never fails to delight. From a distance, it's a mere blur of brilliant blue and orange. Patience and stillness are needed to gain a good close-up view of the kingfisher's fantastic plumage in all its dazzling, iridescent splendour. In spring and summer, you are most likely to see kingfishers on sheltered, tree-lined parts of the Camel. In cold weather, you may find them fishing further down the estuary and nearer the coast. If a kingfisher becomes aware of an observer it's likely to dash away, but it usually returns to continue fishing.

Gaff Wood

If you are at Polbrock, an excursion into Gaff Wood is highly recommended. Owned and managed by the Pencarrow Estate, the wood has been open to the public since 1989. In the past, it was heavily coppiced for charcoal. Today it is regarded by locals as the perfect bluebell woods, and an ideal picnic spot.

In spring, the brilliant colour of the bluebells (*Hyancinthoides non-scriptus*) and the pungent unmistakable whiff of wild garlic (*Allium ursinum*) provide a feast for the senses. If you have brought a picnic, the broad leaf-blades of the wild garlic make a tasty salad accompaniment.

Wild garlic is also known as ramsons. I'm not sure why the plant got this name, but the reason for its common names — stink bombs, stinking nanny, and stinking onions — are obvious. Don't be put off. Individual wild garlic leaves are surprisingly mild and tasty.

Venture into the wood just before the bluebells bloom and you will probably come across the large, white flowers of the wood anemone (*Anemone nemorosa*), also known as grandmother's nightcap. Their presence in such profusion is a sure sign that Gaff is an ancient woodland. Wood anemones are

Bluebells in Gaff Wood

Ramsons in Gaff Wood (facing page).
The Camel meanders below the lower margins of
the wood (above). Wood anemone (left)

notoriously slow to colonize new areas. Seeds are rarely fertile. The plants spread mainly by vegetative reproduction at a rate of no more than 2 metres every 100 years or so.

Plants, fortunately, remain in one place long enough to make observation easy.

Badger (above). Fox cubs (left)

Animals, especially woodland animals, are not so considerate. They usually dart off before you can get a good look at them. Nevertheless, if they are caught by surprise, you might see badgers (*Meles meles*), red deer (*Cervus elaphus*), or a family of foxes (*Vulpes vulpes*) during your excursion. Even if the badgers stay out of sight, their slides, setts and droppings are sure signs that there's a large population in the wood.

Conservation Walks

When you come down on to the Camel Trail from Gaff Wood, you can either turn left and make your way back to Polbrock, or turn right towards Wadebridge. If going back to Polbrock on foot, it's worth taking a diversion along the Conservation Walks and through the unimproved flower-rich water meadows adjoining the river. Armed with a decent pair of binoculars or a telescope, it's also an excellent spot to watch birds.

Early on a summer's evening you are almost guaranteed to see swallows (*Hirundo rustica*) using their amazing aeronautical agility to capture mayfly and other insects emerging from the river. Dippers (*Cinclus cinclus*), short-tailed and rather plump, dip into the river- and stream-beds for shrimp, caddis fly larvae and small fish. And barn owls (*Tyto alba*) sometimes come down to the meadows and marshland before and around dusk to hunt for mice, rats and other rodents hiding in the grass. Although its heart-shaped face has endeared it to many, this owl is an efficient predator. With an ability to fly almost silently, and exceptional hearing, it can locate its prey by sound alone. Once located, the prey is normally ingested whole. Indigestible parts, such as fur and bones, are regurgitated as a blackish pellet.

A barn owl in the marsh

Clockwise from top left: Reed warbler,
sedge warbler and dipper

Other common birds in the meadows and adjacent vegetation are sedge warblers (*Acrocephalus schoenobaenus*) and reed warblers (*Acrocephalus scirpaceus*). Both birds are small, rather undistinguished-looking summer visitors that come from Africa to breed in the reed-beds and other vegetation on the Camel. Although they look very similar at first sight, a sedge warbler has a striking broad, creamy stripe above its eye, while a reed warbler has no such stripe. They also have quite distinct songs. That of a sedge warbler is a noisy, rambling warble; the reed warbler's is more rhythmic.

In the twilight hours, Daubenton's water bats (*Myotis daubentoni*) emerge from their daytime roosts to take their turn at feeding over the water. They tend to choose the calmer stretches, avoiding ripples and anything else that interferes with their powers of echo-location.

Flag irises on the marsh

Gaff Wood to Pendavey Bridge via Shooting Range Platform

The Camel Trail between Gaff Wood and Shooting Range Platform runs almost straight alongside the floodplain, some distance from the river. In summer, the brilliant yellow flowers of the flag iris (*Iris pseudacorus*) stand out against the green of the floodplain's watery margins. Look closely at an iris stalk and you might see a dragonfly or damselfly nymph emerging from its case after a year or two under water. Once its wings are expanded and dried, a dragonfly takes to the air as a brilliantly coloured flyer feeding on any creature it can capture. Adult damselflies are also aerial carnivores, but more delicate and less energetic. And while dragonflies rest with their wings open, damselflies, like the demoiselle (*Calopteryx virgo*), have them closed.

Clockwise from top left: Common darter dragonfly, beautiful demoiselle, mayfly. Water hemlock (facing page)

In June and July, white, umbrella-shaped flower heads of water hemlock (*Oenanthe crocata*) cover much of the flood plain. Toxic alkaloids, designed to deter herbivores, are present in all parts of the plant, making it one of Britain's most poisonous. But because of its parsley-like flower heads, celery-like leaf stalks, and parsnip-like roots, water hemlock has been mistaken for an edible plant, with fatal consequences. Even skin contact with its poisonous sap can cause a painful rash. So this plant must be treated with respect.

From Shooting Range Platform to Pendavey Bridge, the Camel Trail opens up with views of Egloshayle church in the distance. The name of the Platform originates from the time when it was a stop-off point for army marksmen who regularly tested their skill on targets set up across the floodplain on the Treraven side of the valley. Pendavey Bridge passes over the Camel, making it an ideal spot for leaning over and practising the art of Pooh sticks. Looking down the estuary from the bridge, you can also see the grazing land that is being transformed into a dynamic wildlife site.

Pendavey Bridge to Wadebridge, via Guineaport

Some of the land that extends from Slades-bridge to Guineaport is owned by the Gaia Trust, an organization committed to sustainable development and nature conservation. In 1999, Jenni Thomson, the Trust's Director, approached the Environment Agency with the idea of restoring the land to its original salt marsh state. Salt marshes may not look very exciting, but they are precious wildlife habitats. The Agency enthusiastically embraced the idea and gave James Burke, their Freshwater Biodiversity Officer, the challenging job of driving forward the project. When completed, it will be among the largest land restoration projects in Cornwall.

Newly flooded fields at Treraven (above). Egloshayle in frost (facing page)

James is one of the new breed of habitat managers, intent on working with nature rather than against her. With the support of local landowners and financial help from other agencies such as Natural England, he is making the idea become a reality. Pipes have been drilled through the riverbanks opposite Egloshayle church, and drainage ditches and pools dug so that the new salt marsh will be connected to the estuary at high spring tides. Every couple of weeks or so, salt water will flood over the land, and then slowly ebb away, recreating the conditions needed for salt-marsh plants and animals to prosper. If things go as planned, as well as providing a new home for little egrets, mullet and flounder, the reclaimed salt marsh will enhance what is already an AONB (Area of Outstanding Natural Beauty).

Wadebridge

The River Camel flows under three bridges on its way from Wadebridge to Padstow. Just below Guineaport, the Challenge Bridge connects Wadebridge playing fields with the Jubilee Field. Dedicated to the memory of local GP Dr Keith Bailey, the bridge was built in 1991 as part of a television series, 'Challenge Anneka', which was hosted by Anneka Rice. Inevitably, it has acquired the celebrity's name and is usually called 'Anneka's Bridge'.

From the bridge, you can often see mallard ducks (*Anas platyrhincos*). Easily overlooked because of their familiarity, they are worth close observation. There are few birds more beautiful than the drake. The brilliant metallic green of his plumage is best seen on fine spring days when the sun shines low in the sky. This is also the time when males compete for a mate. After courtship, the duck is left to bring up her family alone. Watching the progress of the new brood is a bit like following the trials and tribulations of a television soap opera family. It's not unusual to see people who use the bridge daily stopping half way across to count the ducklings, and expressing great concern if there are any missing. Unfortunately, duckling survival is

Wadebridge from the A39 (facing page).
The Old Bridge (top). Mallard drake (above)

low. Most are taken by gulls, or swept away by a strong tide.

The Old Bridge in the centre of the town was built by the Revd Thomas Lovibond, Vicar of Egloshayle, in 1468. According to legend, the builders had difficulty finding sufficiently strong foundations and solved the problem

Mute swan in flight

Mute swan (*Cygnus olor*)
Mute swans are easily distinguished from other swans by their heavy orange beaks; in adult males, the base is ornamented by a black knob. The male and female work together to build a nest of rushes and reeds. A swan's nest is about 1–2 metres in diameter, and is usually built on a mound within easy access of water. Typically, from five to seven eggs are laid in March to May, and are incubated for about 36 days. A swan's diet consists of a variety of water plants supplemented by small frogs, fish and insects.

(1602) described the bridge as 'the largest, strongest and fairest that the Shire can muster.' Widened in 1853 and 1963, and refurbished in 1994, the number of arches on the bridge has been reduced. Of the original 17 only 13 are now visible. But it is still an impressive structure, greatly revered by bridge enthusiasts and one of the town's treasures.

The bridge is a convenient place to pause and admire some of the river's best-loved wildlife, especially swans, grey mullet and lapwing. Swans are so strongly associated with Wadebridge that one features on the town's coat-of-arms; there's even a popular inn named The Swan, near the Wadebridge end of the bridge.

by using wool-packs. Hence the construction became known as 'the bridge built on wool', or, simply 'the Bridge on Wool'. However it was built, Carew in his *Survey of Cornwall*

Mute swan with cygnets (top). Lapwing (above)

and graceful curve to its long neck, is a majestic sight. On land, it looks like a ballerina wearing wellington boots. Unsurprisingly, as they are such large birds, swans appear to have difficulty taking off and landing. Once in the air, they fly smoothly and quickly, using slow, steady, powerful wing beats. During flight, the primary feathers spread outwards and create a far-reaching, throbbing sound, which may help birds to keep in touch. Despite their name, mute swans can snort, snore and grunt. However, their calls lack the musical quality of the trumpeting and crooning sounds made by other swans.

Be wary when approaching a swan. Adults, especially males, are highly aggressive. When approached, they fluff their neck feathers, lay their head back and hiss their displeasure as they swim jerkily but purposefully towards an intruder.

From September through to spring, the delightful lapwing (*Vanellus vanellus*) takes up temporary residence on the estuary. Adults are easily identified by their long crest. At low tide, they can often be seen close to the bridge, probing their beaks into muddy sand for ragworm and other small animals. Although common on mudflats, this is not a wader but a bird of pastures and ploughed fields. It breeds on Bodmin Moor and at

Mute swans (*Cygnus olor*) nest on the small islands close to the bridge. Elevated mounds have been specially constructed on the islands so that a nest can be built out of the reach of high spring tides. On water, a swan with its brilliant white plumage, round head

Grey mullet

Thick-lipped grey mullet (*Chelon labrosus*)
The thick-lipped grey mullet is the commonest species of mullet in the Camel. This coastal fish moves into the estuary, and even into the fresh water of the river, on a rising tide. It feeds on zooplankton, bottom-living organisms and detritus. It can grow up to 75 cm long and can live for 16 years.

Amble, coming to the estuary when foraging in fields is difficult. Lapwings are active birds that require ready access to a good source of suitable food. At high tide, they rest on the island upriver from the bridge, uttering the occasional 'peet-p-weet peewit peewit' that gives them their other common name. Vulnerable to habitat change, populations of lapwing on Bodmin Moor are in decline. So it's important that they can make a good living on the Camel during the winter months.

Under the bridge, shoals of thick-lipped grey mullet (*Chelon labrosus*) feed, pig-like, with their snouts in the mud. If you have a sensitive disposition, it's best not to enquire too closely into what they eat; suffice it to say that grey mullet do particularly well close to sewage outfalls.

When in shallow water, the fish look tantalizingly close and easy to catch. However, these 'grey ghosts' of the riverbed are exceedingly elusive of bait and hook. Even so, in summer the river banks are often lined with anglers attracted by the challenge of catching the fish that is said to become 'turbocharged' when disturbed. If the intention is to fish for food rather than sport, grey mullet taken from around the bridge can be a disappointment unless cooked well in garlic and wine; those caught at sea taste better.

Wadebridge to the Slate Quarries, via Amble Salt Marshes and Tregunna Mudflats

Downstream from Lovibond's bridge, the by-pass bridge provides a modern thoroughfare for traffic along the Atlantic Highway. Salt marshes are the dominant feature below the bridge. They are vital to the Camel ecosystem, acting as nursery grounds, food sources, sediment sinks and flood buffers. Those at Amble are particularly important for wildfowl. The marshes are a complex mosaic of narrow creeks, islands of vegetation and small, isolated areas of bare mud, known as salt pans.

Salt pans experience wild swings in salt content. After filling with seawater at high spring tides, they can become exceptionally salty when they dry out, or highly diluted after heavy rainfall. Such variations in salt content are unsuitable for most animals. Nevertheless, fish fry often become trapped in the pans, making them excellent snacking areas

Trewornan marshes

Glasswort

Sea purslane

Glasswort (*Salicornia* species)
Glasswort is a succulent plant, usually less than 30 cm high. It is highly tolerant of salt, surviving complete submersion in seawater. It can be eaten raw or cooked. It is particularly tasty as a fish accompaniment when steamed and coated in butter. However, like all herbs collected from the wild, it needs careful washing before being eaten. In former times, glasswort was burnt as a source of soda for glass-making.

Sea purslane (*Halimione portulacoides*)
This bushy perennial grows up to 1 m high. Its greyish-green leaves are salty and fleshy to conserve precious water. They become silvery in bright sunlight, minimizing the risk of scorching. The yellowish flower spikes appear between July and October. Like glasswort, sea purslane is an excellent accompaniment to seafood. Its crunchy and salty leaves cooked with creamy scallops have been described as 'a match made in heaven', and the taste of its succulent pods is said to 'explode on the tongue'.

Cord grass colony

Walmsley tower hide

for little egrets (*Egretta garzetta*) and herons (*Ardea cinerea*).

Conspicuous mats of green seaweeds grow in the pans at certain times of the year, with millions of microscopic photosynthesizing organisms called diatoms. Diatoms are highly pigmented, turning the mud yellow, brown or green, depending on their colour.

Salt marshes grow out of bare, estuarine mud. One of the early colonizers is glasswort (*Salicornia* species). Its roots trap sediment, encouraging the growth of other salt-tolerant plants.

Another early colonizer is cord grass (*Spartina* species). This has started to grow on the Tregunna mudflats, threatening to turn them into salt marsh. As the mudflats are important feeding grounds for waders, the cord grass has been cut back and removed to prevent it from spreading.

The edges of established salt marshes are eroded by the tides to form salting cliffs. These are more than one metre high in some places, and mark the upper limit of neap tides. Below the cliffs there is bare mud; above them is a dense sward of salt-marsh plants dominated by sea purslane and scurvy grass (*Cochlearaia officinalis*).

The mud below the salt marshes is gooey, but exceptionally rich in microscopic organisms. These provide an almost limitless source of food for two of the must successful exploiters of Tregunna mud: a bivalve – the peppery furrow shell (*Scrobicularia plana*) – and mudsnails (*Hydrobia ulvae*). Both are important food items for waders. Curlews

Mudsnails on peppery furrow shell

Peppery furrow shell (*Scrobicularia plana*)

Empty shells scattered on the foreshore of Tregunna are evidence of a large population of *Scrobicularia plana* living deep in the mud. These bivalves have two separate siphons which extend upwards through the mud. One siphon takes in water as a source of oxygen. The other probes the surface of the mud like a miniature elephant's trunk, grabbing nutritious morsels of food, which it then sucks down into its stomach. This second siphon leaves characteristic star-shaped marks on the surface of the mud. Adults lie at depths of about 20 cm, well beyond the reach of any wader's bill. Only the younger bivalves living in shallower burrows are vulnerable to predation by birds. But any siphons protruding up into the water are in danger of being cropped by small fish fry, such as flounder (*Platichthys flesus*), that use the estuary as a nursery.

Mudsnail (*Hydrobia ulvae*)

Each mudsnail is only the size of a single grain of rice. What mudsnails lack in size, they gain in numbers. On the mud near Dinham, densities average about 10,000 per square metre, but in places they can exceed 60,000 per square metre. Mudsnails are so successful because they can exploit different food sources. At low tide they crawl on the mud, eating diatoms and green weeds. On a flood tide, they make a mucus raft from which they are carried up the shore. The mucus also acts as a net in which food is trapped. When the snail detaches from the raft, early on an ebb tide, it sinks to the bottom and eats the food-laden mucus.

Because of their astronomical numbers, mudsnails are regarded by many estuarine biologists as the most important animal that you can see on the mud. They form a large proportion of the diet of shelduck (*Tadorna tadorna*).

(*Numenius arquata*), with their long beaks, can capture young bivalves in their burrows, while plovers and other short-beaked birds make do with surface-dwelling mudsnails.

The Camel Estuary is renowned for its variety of overwintering waders. Those on the Tregunna mudflats can be observed from the public hide just off the Camel Trail.

Another excellent bird-watching site is the fabulous tower hide on the Walmsley

Clockwise from top left: Male shelduck, Canada goose, curlew

Shelduck (*Tadoma tadoma*)

A shelduck is easy to identify. It has a dark, iridescent green head and neck, a broad band of chestnut across its breast, and black primary feathers contrasting with its general white plumage. A small population breeds on the Camel. This is boosted by overwintering birds. Numbers commonly exceed 300 in January. Shelduck upend in shallow water to feed on mudsnails, or they scuttle for them on the mud when the tide is low.

Sanctuary, opened in 1999 by Bill Oddie, the bearded birdie of 'The Goodies' fame. The sanctuary, managed by the Cornwall Bird-Watching and Preservation Society (CBWPS), includes over 20 ha of pasture reclaimed from Amble salt marshes. Estuarine species seen from the hide include golden plover (*Pluvialis apricaria*), greenshank (*Tringa nebularia*), black-tailed godwit (*Limosa limosa*) and dunlin (*Calidris alpina*), as well as large numbers of wigeon (*Anas penelope*) and other wildfowl. Flocks of Canada geese (*Branta canadensis*) – a species introduced from North America – can also be seen grazing vegetation here and on other parts of the estuary. (For access to the hide, contact CBWPS via their website: www.cbwps.org.uk.)

From top: Black-tailed godwits, greenshank, dunlin at dawn

The Slate Quarries

The extensive piles of broken rubble that lie about half way between Wadebridge and Padstow are the remnants of the millions of tonnes of slate cut over a period of hundreds of years for the Penquean and Camel Quarries. The quarries closed in the 1890s, before the advent of the railway line to Padstow.

Camel Quarry old quay

Those of us brought up with the Cornish coat of arms on our school exercise books, have an indelible image of miners and fishermen in our brains. We tend to look back with nostalgia at the 'good old days', when mining brought prosperity to the county, forgetting how hard the times were for ordinary miners. Slate quarrymen at the Penquean and Camel worked in pits down to about 90 metres below sea level. Imagine what it must have been like in those dark and dank conditions. No doubt, on reaching the surface at the end of a back-breaking shift, they would have been greatly relieved to be able to take deep

Cant Hill

Buzzard (left). Cock kestrel (right)

Buzzard (*Buteo buteo*)

Buzzards are our most common bird of prey, and the one you are most likely to see over Cant Hill. They soar with wings straight and motionless, tips of primary feathers curved upwards and tails spread out.

Buzzards hunt during the day, usually on their own. With eyes set close together to maximize stereoscopic vision, the ability of a beady-eyed buzzard to sight and attack its prey from a distance is mind-boggling. It has an incredible 1,000,000 light receptors per square millimetre of retina, compared with our 200,000, giving it six to eight times better distance vision. Once it has caught sight of its target, a buzzard drops quickly down. With sharp, strong talons extended, it grabs the victim, and then rips the flesh from the body with its hooked beak. There can be few sights more fearsome to a small mammal than the shadow of one of these birds passing overhead. When not in the air, buzzards spend much of their time perching on posts or in trees, looking out for potential prey.

gulps of revitalizing, clean Camel air, and have their spirits raised by the magnificent views of the nearby estuary and its wildlife.

Although cyclists and walkers have replaced the miners at the quarry head, the views are still magnificent. Opposite the quarry is Cant Hill. It rises high above the estuary, forcing warm air upwards and creating the thermals used to great effect by birds of prey such as buzzards (*Buteo buteo*), kestrel (*Falco tinnunculus*) and peregrine (*Falco peregrinus*).

On rare occasions, osprey (*Pandion haliaetus*) have been sighted snatching sea bass from the estuary. Satellite tracking indicates that these birds are probably Scottish juveniles, refuelling before continuing their journey south over the dangerous Bay of Biscay.

Osprey

To the right of Cant Hill, you can see what remains of a windmill – one of more than 30 which, in the past, serviced a thriving wheat-growing area. Today, wheat is grown only on the lower slopes of Cant Hill. Some of the upper parts are grazed. Much of the steeper slopes are festooned with the yellow flowers of furze, or common gorse (*Ulex europeaus*). This green and spiny plant bears some brilliant yellow flowers at most times of the year, giving rise to the catchphrase, 'When gorse is out of blossom, kissing's out of season.'

When the gorse is dried out by a hot summer sun, it has a notorious reputation as a potential fire hazard. It burns so ferociously that it was once used as a fuel in bakers' ovens. Fortunately, gorse is well adapted to periodic conflagrations. Its seedpods are opened by extreme heat, allowing rapid regeneration after fire. Without regular fires, gorse becomes replaced by taller-growing trees, unless wind-pruning or some other factor excludes the competing plants.

Soils on the slate and shale scree are thin. This has allowed shallow-rooting species such as orchids to grow, without the danger of being swamped by grasses and other fast-growing, deep-rooting vegetation. There are two orchids common at the Quarry and along some parts of the Camel Trail: the spring-flowering early purple orchid (*Orchis mascula*), and later-flowering pyramidal orchid (*Anacamptis pyramidalis*). Another plant that does well at the Quarry is the little robin (*Geranium purpuruem*). In Britain, this

Early purple orchid (top). Common lizard (above)

relatively rare species only grows in the extreme south-west.

One of the animals that frequents the quarry is the common lizard (*Lacerta vivipara*). On summer mornings, it can sometimes be seen sunbathing on a piece of slate before going off in search of food. Being a so-called 'cold-blooded' reptile, it cannot move swiftly until the blood going through its muscles has warmed up.

Early purple orchid (*Orchis mascula*)
Orchids are usually associated with steamy, tropical environments, but the early purple thrives in the mild and moist climate of the Camel Estuary. In most years, dozens can be seen in flower at the Slate Quarry. The exquisitely shaped flowers, usually purple, sometimes pink or white, appear between April and June. The two sepals have been described as 'being held like the wings of an angel', with markings on individual flowers having the appearance of a little face. Unfortunately, the older flowers are far from angelic, giving off a strong and unpleasant smell that brings to mind tomcat urine. The early purple orchid is so-called because it is the first of our orchids to flower in the yearly cycle. Its other common name, the purple spotted orchid, derives from the dark spots or blotches that appear on the glossy green leaves of most (but not all) of the plants. Like all British orchids, the early purple has tuberous roots, whose shape gave the genus its name (in Latin, *orchis* means testicle). In Turkey and some other Eastern countries, the tubers (dried and powdered, then mixed with milk or water and sweetened with honey) are used to make *sahlep*, a wholesome and nutritious drink. In eighteenth-century London, before tea and coffee became popular beverages, such a drink was sold in special Salopian shops.

The Slate Quarries to Padstow, via Pinkson and Little Petherick Creeks

A short distance from the Quarries is Pinkson Creek, the site of a large heronry. Of all the birds in the world, the grey heron is my personal favourite. I am always captivated by the way it seeks its prey. A picture of total concentration, neck outstretched, it strides stealthily in shallow water, stopping as still as a garden statue when it catches a glimpse of something moving below. With one leg in the water and the other half raised, it is poised to

Grey heron at nest

Grey heron (*Ardea cinerea*)
Grey herons are a common sight feeding in the Camel, from the brackish creeks and estuarine channels at low tide, to the fresh-water streams above Polbrock. Food includes fish, frogs, rats, beetles, and even small birds. Every year since at least the 1960s, the trees at the back of Pinkson Creek have supported up to 18 stick-and-reed nests. Each nest bears between three and five light blue eggs. The eggs, laid between February and May, are incubated for about 25 days, and the young leave the nest after seven or eight weeks.

attack. If it sees a potential meal, it will make a lightning-fast strike, stabbing downwards at its target with its pickaxe beak.

Another member of the heron family that nests in a creek on the Camel is the little egret (*Egretta garzetta*). It has bright white plumage feathers, with a contrasting black bill, black legs and yellow feet. Its long plumes were once regarded as such a desirable fashion item, that the little egret was nearly persecuted to extinction.

The little egret first made its appearance on the Camel Estuary as a rare spring vagrant. In the 1990s it remained a non-breeding visitor from mainland Europe. Numbers peaked

Pinkson Creek (facing page). Little Petherick Creek and Sea Mills (top). Little egret (above)

Birdwatchers on the Camel Trail

at about 80 in the late summer and early autumn, following dispersal from breeding colonies. Since then, the Camel population has become large enough for these gregarious birds to take up permanent residence. In 2006 about six pairs nested in the estuary.

Little egret eat mainly small fish from streams and pools, but they will also take ragworm from the mud. One of the best places to sit and enjoy the feeding antics of these lively hunters is at the hamlet of Sea Mills, in the creek that leads to Little Petherick.

Before you reach Little Petherick along the Camel Trail, you have to go over the old railway bridge at Oldtown Cove, and past the wreck on the beach. On the other side of the estuary is Gentle Jane, an isolated little place whose name has generated much speculation. According to one legend, an old lady once lived there who was involved in various dubious activities, including sheltering smugglers. Perhaps the 'gentle' is ironic, like 'little' in Little John.

Little Petherick Creek has an extensive area of mudflats connected to the rest of the estuary by a narrow and shallow tidal channel. Its fine, silty upper shore is a favourite site for redshank (*Tringa totanus*) feeding on a tiny crustacean called *Corophium*. Redshank capture these tunnelling cousins to the sand hopper by pecking just beneath the sediment surface at rates of up to 100 pecks per minute, or by sweeping their bill from side to side over the silt. When temperatures are low, *Corophium* become inactive and lie deeper in the sediment. Then redshank resort to feeding on ragworm or molluscs in the mud, or move inland to take earthworms and leatherjackets. When disturbed, redshank have a reputation for taking to the air and calling hysterically. This behaviour has earned them the title 'sentinels of the marshes'.

The main crossing point of Little Petherick Creek is the Iron Bridge. The mud and silty sand beneath the bridge is a favourite place for bait diggers to search for ragworm (*Hediste diversicolor*) or lugworm (*Arenicola marina*). Both are marine bristle worms (polychaetes). Ragworm are heavy-jawed hunters, able to move freely over the substrate in search of food. They have a varied diet. Large specimens have been seen in salt pans, seizing the dying young of grey mullet, and dragging them head-first into the mud.

While ragworm leave their burrows to make feeding excursions, lugworm lead more sedentary lives. They rarely come out of their subterranean home.

A lugworm lives in an L-shaped burrow. It draws water into one end, creating a conical depression in the surface of the sand. Food carried in the water is trapped between sand particles, which the lugworm eats. Undigest-

Old railway bridge, Oldtown Cove (top).
Iron Bridge (above)

ed material is ejected at the other end of the burrow as the familiar worm caste.

Lugworm and ragworm are not only useful to anglers. They occur in such enormous numbers on the Camel that they form an important part of the diet of many of the estuary's fish and birds.

From top: Ragworm, lugworm, cockles

Extending 2,000 metres from the Iron Bridge to Padstow Harbour, and 900 metres across the estuary towards Rock and Porthilly, is Town Bar, a large inter-tidal sandbank cut by water channels. Its margins consist of smooth mounds of sand deposited during ebb tides. The bulk of the Bar has its surface scoured twice a day by floodtides, creating an ever-changing pattern of sand waves. Underneath the mass of sediment live countless cockles (*Cerastoderma edule*). As well as finding their way into seafood dishes, these meaty, filter-feeding bivalves are a favoured food of oystercatchers and other estuarine animals.

Cockling has been a popular pursuit of Padstonians for centuries. Traditional, small-scale hand harvesting using a bucket and rake has little impact on the population. However, in 1996, commercial fishermen started harvesting cockles from boats, using powerful suction dredges. Their 'hoovering up' of the cockles was so efficient that it threatened the survival of local stocks. To protect the cockle, new byelaws were introduced. These restricted cockling to non-mechanical methods only, and set the legal minimum cockle size at 20 mm. Under the byelaws, the Environment Agency also has the power to close the cockle beds if stocks fall below critical levels.

Padstow

In summer, hundreds of thousands of people flock to Padstow to enjoy fine food, stunning scenery, and exhilarating water sports. The harbour – once one of the most important in England – is a safe haven for mariners and fishermen. Luxurious cabin cruisers and bulky beam trawlers moor alongside Cornish crabbers and luggers.

Padstow would not deserve the title of 'active fishing harbour' without its gulls. More than a dozen species have been recorded in and around the Camel, but the herring gull (*Larus argentatus*), with an orange-red spot on its beak, is the most familiar, and certainly the noisiest. Even out of sight, they make their presence known by their raucous calls.

Herring gulls are supreme opportunists, able to take advantage of the leftovers of human activity, scavenging behind fishing boats, rummaging among refuse tips, or poking into bin bags. They have become particularly adept at gathering up scraps left by picnickers on the quayside. A piece of fish thrown carelessly to the ground will transform a herring gull from a serene 'symbol of the seaside' to a ravenous, wildly flapping beast, swooping down on its target like something out of Alfred Hitchcock's horror film *The Birds*. Woe betide anyone who tries to retrieve the fallen morsel. These birds have become so brazen that they are quite capable of snatching food from polystyrene trays opened incautiously within striking distance.

Another gull that you are likely to see in the air above Padstow is the great black-backed

Padstow Town Bar

Clockwise from top left: Great black-backed gull, herring gull on nest, herring gull chick hatching

gull (*Larus marinus*). These gulls are the real bullies of the family. They can grow as large as a goose, and have an appetite to match their size. As well as being carrion eaters, they are accomplished assassins, killing birds and mammals up to the size of a shag or rabbit. If the prey is small, such as a gull chick, they swallow it whole; if too large to swallow, the gulls turn their prey inside out, so that they can eat the tender flesh and avoid the tough skin and feathers. Great black-backed gulls tend to nest singly on the top of rocky outcrops, and on small offshore islands.

Despite dwindling fish stocks and reduced quotas, Padstow still has an active quayside industry that processes and handles fish and shellfish landed by its boats. Several small boats specialize in taking visitors on trips,

A fishing boat enters Padstow harbour

fishing for pollack (*Pollachius pollachius*) off wrecks and reefs, and for mackerel (*Scomber scombus*) in the mouth of the estuary.

The best time to go mackerel fishing is during the summer. At that time of year, mackerel feed intensively on prawns and young fish. They readily take bait that look anything like their prey. In winter, mackerel stop feeding. Adults spend the cold months off the Scottish coast, returning to Cornish waters to spawn in the early spring.

A mackerel is exquisitely adapted for life as a predator of the open sea. Strong muscles running down its back move its crescent-shaped tailfin powerfully from side to side, propelling it swiftly through the water. A mackerel in motion is no 'cold fish'; its muscular activity generates sufficient heat to keep its blood at a temperature several degrees higher than that of the surrounding seawater. Its torpedo-shaped body, lack of swim-bladder, and ability to collapse its dorsal fins, minimize resistance to movement and maximize swimming efficiency. Being without a gas-filled swim-bladder, a mackerel sinks quickly to the bottom when not swimming. But when swimming, its oil-rich tissues provide sufficient buoyancy for it to maintain its mid-water position with ease.

Protein-rich muscles, and tissues soaked in essential fatty acids, make mackerel a highly nutritious and tasty food. It is even tastier if you catch it yourself and cook it fresh on a beach barbecue (authorized, of course).

Sea bass (*Dicentrarchus labrax*) is another streamlined predator that stalks the waters of the Camel. Donovan Kelley, a retired civil servant living at Trebetherick, is the doyen of sea-bass fishing in the South West. As well as being a keen and skilful angler, he has also contributed as much as anyone to our knowledge of the fish's natural history.

Working with scientists from the Marine Biological Association in Plymouth, fellow anglers and commercial fishermen, Don has tagged and aged thousands of fish, monitored their movements, and found out about their population biology. He found that early each summer, thousands of silvery young sea bass enter the Camel Estuary to feed on sand eels, smaller fish and prawns. This information identified the estuary as an important nursery area, and resulted in legislation to conserve bass stocks. For example, fishing by boat for sea bass in the waters behind Stepper Point and Pentire Point is banned from 30 April to 1 December. And anglers are only allowed to keep fish that measure more than 37.5 cm from snout to tip of tail. In 1983 Don's work earned him the Bass Anglers Sporting Society's W. Rawles Memorial Award for outstanding endeavour towards the conservation of sea bass.

Padstow is renowned for its seafood. In addition to succulent sea bass steamed to perfection, you are likely to see dishes of mussels, lobsters and oysters featuring on the menus of Padstow's fine restaurants.

Mussels free from any contamination, and properly prepared, have excellent health-giving properties. They are extremely high in proteins, calcium and iron, and low in fat and calories. They are reputed to be good for your heart, with high amounts of omega-3s (fatty acids believed to lower blood pressure). They are also one of the easiest, tastiest and most economical shellfish to enjoy.

Mussels are filter-feeding bivalves. Extensive beds dominate many of North Cornwall's rocky shores. To prevent waves and tides sweeping them away, mussels attach themselves to a suitable solid surface by a mass of fine threads that form the familiar 'beard'. They use iron from the sea as a binding agent to make a 'superglue' which they secrete at the end of each thread. This natural glue is so strong and waterproof, that it is being developed as a non-toxic, environment-friendly alternative to artificial, formaldehyde-based adhesives. Jonathan Wilker, a chemistry professor, is particularly excited about its potential use as a surgical adhesive, inspiring ScienCentral Video News to report, 'Wouldn't it be great if instead of sewing you up, surgeons could glue you back together?'

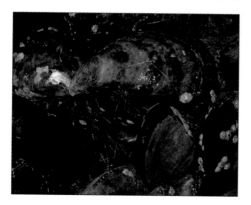

Padstow Mussels

Most of the Camel's mussels are not *Mytilus edulis*, the usual species on Britain's shores, but *Mytilus galloprovincialis*, a species more commonly found in France and the Mediterranean. The Gallic mussel has become such a strong feature of the town that it is known as the Padstow Mussel.

Lobsters (*Homarus gammarus*) are the giants of British crustacea. According to the *Guinness Book of Records*, the largest European lobster measured 1.26 metres and weighed 9.3 kg (20 lb 8 oz), and was caught on the Fowey in 1931. Most lobsters captured in pots off Padstow weigh no more than a couple of kilograms (5 lb), but if not caught they normally grow to over 5 kg (11 lb), and can live for more than 20 years.

The best place to get a close-up view of a live lobster is in the National Lobster Hatchery on Padstow's South Quay. One price of Padstow's success as a seafood centre is the increasing demand for freshly caught lobsters. This has put local stocks at risk. The Hatchery was set up to help lobster fishermen sustain their industry. Pregnant lobsters are brought into the hatchery. After the eggs hatch, the young are nurtured through several juvenile stages in conditions carefully controlled by Dom Boothroyd and his staff. Lobsters are cannibalistic, so contact between individuals

Young lobsters at the National Lobster Hatchery

must be kept to a minimum to prevent high fatalities. The earliest, free-floating stages are grown in specially designed water-filled vessels through which air is bubbled to reduce contact between individuals. Older, bottom-living stages are isolated in individual compartments, fed a good diet, and kept until they are large enough to be released back into the wild. On average, only a couple of the many thousand eggs carried by a hen lobster would survive the trials and tribulations of larval life in the open sea. With the tender care of the Hatchery staff, about two out of ten should make it to adulthood, to boost local stocks.

To see the Camel's oysters, take a short ferry trip across the estuary to Rock, and go from there to Porthilly. On that side of the estuary you can explore the shores and cliffs up to Pentire Point and the Rumps.

Rock and Porthilly

Magnificent views of giant dunes greet passengers on the ferry as it crosses from Padstow to Rock. Cassock Hill, rising about 50 metres above the landing point, towers above the beach and gives a kestrel's eye-view of the lower dunes and the fairways of St Enodoc golf course. The Hill, as with all the high dunes, is made of Devonian slate overlain with wind-driven sand. Close examination reveals that the sand contains fragments of the shells that once protected whelks, scallops, cockles and many other types of marine mollusc living in the estuary and nearby coastal waters.

Padstow–Rock ferry and sand dunes

Clockwise from top left: Evening primrose, pyramidal orchid, kidney vetch, greater knapweed, viper's bugloss, sea bindweed, field scabious, restharrow

Sand is a good source of calcium, so the dunes support an extremely rich flora of calcium-loving plants. These include red fescue (*Festuca rubra*, the grass that makes up much of the turf on the dunes), kidney vetch (*Anthyllis vuleraria*), wild thyme (*Thymus preacox*), sea bindweed (*Calystegia soldanella*) and pyramidal orchids (*Anacamptis pyramidalis*). Other common plants seen on the dunes and adjacent fields are restharrow (*Ononis repens*), field scabious (*Knautia arvensis*), and the thistle-like greater knapweed (*Centaurea scabiosa*).

In summer, one of the most striking plants flowering on the dunes is evening primrose (*Oenothera sp*). At dusk, its large, sweet-

Clockwise from top left: Marbled white butterfly, ringlet butterfly, six-spot burnet moth, common blue butterfly

smelling yellow flowers open to visits from night-flying moths which pollinate them. This flower opening is triggered by a drop in light intensity, and happens in a matter of seconds – a remarkably quick response for a plant.

Among the rarer plants on the dunes are grey-hair grass (*Corynephorus canescens*), yellow wort (*Blackstonia perfoliata*), Portland spurge (*Euphorbia portlandica*) and viper's-bugloss (*Echium vulgare*). The last is a herb with curved sprays of brilliant blue flowers. It acquired its name from being used as a cure for snake-bite.

As well as bringing a dash of colour to the dunes during their flowering seasons, the flora support a huge number of small invertebrates. The large community of dune molluscs includes the pointed or conical snail

(*Cochlicella acuta*), the wrinkled dune snail (*Candidula intersecta*) and the banded snail (*Cernuella virgata*). Among the numerous butterflies are the marbled white (*Menargia galathea*), ringlets (*Aphantopus hyperantus*), and common blue (*Polyommatus icarus*). One of the moths found on the dunes is the day-flying six-spot burnet (*Zygaena filipendulae*). Its has blackish forewings highlighted by bright red spots: these colours are a warning to potential predators that it is poisonous.

Another notable insect inhabiting the dunes is the striking great green bush cricket (*Tettigonia viridissima*). Growing up to 5.4 cm long, it is the largest cricket in the UK. Males are often heard before being seen. By raising their wings and rubbing them together, they produce the high-pitched trilling sounds with which they serenade females. Great green bush crickets are endowed with an impressive set of mouth parts. They use these to bite off bits of plants and other insects, and to chew them thoroughly. Be warned! They will also nip a finger if given half a chance.

Between Rock and Brea Hill, a raised beach separates the sand dunes from the present shore line. Its cliff of stabilized sand is perforated with holes: small ones made by sand wasps, and larger ones by rabbits and sand martins. In crevices and between slabs of

Great green bush cricket (top).
Rock samphire (above)

slate, salt-tolerant rock samphire (*Crithmum maritinum*) abounds. Just above the sandy shore on slate surfaces sheltered from wave action, maritime mosses (*Grimmia maritima*) form rigid, yellowish-green cushions.

A short distance up the estuary from Rock is Porthilly. In the sixteenth century it was a busy hamlet and harbour (Porthilly means 'harbour on the estuary'). St Michael's, the

Marram grass dune stabilization (top).
Tamarisk towards St Enodoc (above)

The Rock Sand Dune Community

The dunes at Rock contain a succession of plant communities from the top of the shore towards the land. Scattered along the strandline are pioneering plants such as the nationally rare sea spurge (*Euphorbia paralias*), annual sea blite (*Suaeda maritima*) and sea rocket (*Cakile maritima*). Just above these, still regularly splashed by the sea, are embryonic dunes dominated by the salt-tolerant dune builder sand couch grass (*Agropyron junceiforme*). Further inland, where enough nutrients have accumulated from dead and decaying pioneering plants, is marram grass (*Ammophila arenaria*). Its extensive network of underground stems helps to bind sand, stabilizing it and preparing it for colonization by other grasses and perennial flowering plants. Further inland still, where the dunes are stable, gorse and blackthorn scrub dominate.

One bushy shrub sure to catch the eye on the dunes leading to St Enodoc church is tamarisk (*Tamarix gallica*). Its fresh green, feathery branches suggest an exotic origin. It was first introduced during Tudor times, probably from Germany, to treat disorders of the liver and spleen. Today, because of its salt tolerance, it is planted on many exposed, sandy beaches of North Cornwall as a windbreak and screening or hedging plant. It is extremely easy to propagate. In winter, just cut a piece the size of a walking stick, sharpen its base, drive it into the ground, and the following spring a new plant will sprout.

Raised beach at Rock (left). Sand martin (right)

Sand martins (*Riparia riparia*)

Sand martins are not exclusively maritime; among the other places they live are steep riverbanks, railway cuttings, and old sandpits. Arriving at Rock in early spring, they either make use of last year's holes, or excavate new burrows. The burrows are about a metre deep, and end in a chamber lined with grass and feathers, on which four or five white eggs are laid. The eggs are incubated mainly by the female, and hatch in a fortnight. Hatching is followed by a fledging period of about three weeks. Like their close relatives the swallows and house martins, sand martins are aerial feeders. Both parents feed insects to the young, usually catching their prey over water. After about 19 days, the young take to the air and work on their flying skills by performing intricate aerobatics. These often involve chasing a feather carried by one of the parent birds. Normally two broods are produced before September, when most sand martins leave to winter in the Sahel region of North Africa.

little church just above the beach, was much used by seafarers. Today, with the bay made shallow by heavy silting, Porthilly has lost its status as a harbour, but it is still used as a safe mooring for small boats.

On the foreshore between Porthilly and Cant Hill, Tim Marshall has been farming an oyster of oriental origin, *Crassostrea gigas*, for more than 20 years. Sometimes called the Pacific Oyster or Japanese Oyster, this

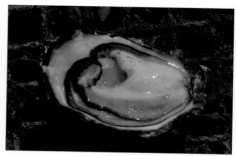

Tim Marshall at his oyster beds (left).
Open Pacific oyster (above)

crinkly-shelled bivalve is much faster growing than the native oyster (*Ostrea edulis*), for which Helford is famous.

The Pacific oysters start their life on the Camel as small seed, each about the size of a fingernail. They are grown in meshed trays on a long line of trestles positioned low down the shore to maximize their feeding time under water. After about a year, when they have reached marketable size, they are transported a short but noisy tractor ride to

Porthilly Farm. Here, Tim has a barn especially equipped to sort and grade the tonnes of oysters he grows every year. So successful is Tim's enterprise that he has been awarded a grant from Objective One through South West Pesca Ltd., to extend his farm. On receiving the award, Tim said, 'My aim is to grow oysters with a high quality shell shape and meat content, and I am always looking for ways to improve survival rates. The extra money will help me produce an even better oyster, and will enable me to compete even though we are a bit removed from the market place here on the Camel.'

When I first met Tim tending the oysters, it was a cloudless day in July. With the sun shining on his back and a gentle sea breeze cooling his face, the life of a shellfisherman

Oystercatcher (left). Turnstone (right)

seemed idyllic. Tim soon dispelled any romantic notions, however, telling me how backbreaking and cold-numbing the work can be in mid-winter. Oyster seed takes about a year to grow to marketable size. No matter what the season or weather, young oysters have to be carefully nurtured, even if this means fingers become frost-nipped from freeing the trays of fouling seaweeds. Nevertheless, Tim revels in his work. He also takes great delight in observing the antics of the birds that share the estuary with his oysters.

Two birds that rarely fail to entertain are turnstones (*Arenaria interpres*) and oystercatchers (*Haemotopus ostralegus*). In winter, the slate shingle beach at Porthilly is an ideal place to see turnstones showing off the unique skills that gave them their name. Running energetically from one spot to another,

a turnstone uses its short black bill and strong neck muscles to flick over pieces of slate and snatch whatever food is underneath.

Oystercatchers are one of the most distinctive residents of the estuary. Their fluty 'kileep' call, black and white plumage, pink legs and orange-red bill, have earned them the name 'pied pipers of the coast'.

Paradoxically, modern oystercatchers rarely feed on oysters, even when they are readily available. In winter, some birds flock to Egloshayle park to probe under the grass for earthworms and other soil invertebrates. But those on the estuary feed mainly on cockles, mussels, limpets and shore crabs. When feeding on bivalves, an oystercatcher uses its bill either to stab through the gaps of the valves, or to hammer the shell repeatedly until it gains access to the meaty flesh.

Daymer Bay to Polzeath

Daymer Bay is a beautiful inlet only a short walk along the sandy shore from Rock. The poet Sir John Betjeman, who spent many summers at nearby Trebetherick, and whose last resting place is in the churchyard behind the Bay, loved this particular seaside. In his autobiography *Summoned by Bells*, he writes of 'the long low stretch from Padstow to Stepper on the other side of the estuary' … 'the scent of seaweed and salty sand', and 'larks and oyster-catchers shrill and small, and sea-gulls wailing like angry babies.' The sights, smells and sounds of the area made this his 'home for the eyes, nose and ears.'

Daymer Bay, Pentire and Newland

Rough sea at Greenaway, looking towards Newland

Among Sir John's favourite places were the rocky shores of Greenaway and Trebetherick Point, between Daymer and Polzeath. Here, school children do much the same today as did Sir John in his childhood. Armed with buckets and nets, they go in search of crabs, fish and other animals.

While the edible crab (*Cancer pagurus*) wedges itself in narrow crevices low down the shore, several species of crab scavenge in the rock pools. The common green shore crab (*Carcinus maenas*) and the feisty and fearless velvet swimming crab (*Necora puber*) are two. If you peer into a pool and see a shell moving much faster than snail pace, it is probably occupied by another type of crab, the hermit crab (*Pagurus bernhardus*). Unlike shore crabs, a hermit crab doesn't bother to make its own hard carapace to cover its soft abdominal tissues. Instead it uses the shell of a dead marine snail, usually a dogwhelk or periwinkle. As it grows, it has to vacate its temporary accommodation and find a new, larger shell.

Sir John Betjeman's headstone in St Enodoc churchyard (left). Shanny or blenny (above)

One of the most common fish found in rock pools, or curled up in crevices, is the shanny or blenny (*Blennius pholis*). It is very well adapted to inter-tidal life and the twice-daily risk of being out of water. If stranded on a rock, it can use its pectoral fins to crawl back into a pool. It can survive out of water for more than a day, breathing through its body surface as long as this is kept moist. To cope with being battered by waves, its scales are deeply embedded under skin made slippery by secretions from mucus glands.

Because its skin is smooth with no scales to be ripped off, a blenny is not particularly prone to being damaged when handled. However, if disturbed, an adrenaline surge causes dark pigments to enlarge, making the fish appear black, aggressive, and more inclined to attack an intruder. Males are distinguished from females by having large, canine-like teeth in the upper jaw, which can inflict a sharp nip on fingers exploring crevices.

Sea anemones, with their stem-like body and brilliantly coloured tentacles, are often mistaken for plants. Yet they are actually car-nivorous animals. They capture their prey by killing them with poisons secreted by spe-cial stinging cells in their tentacles. Beadlets (*Actinia* species) and snakelocks (*Anemonia viridis*) are two of the commonest anemones

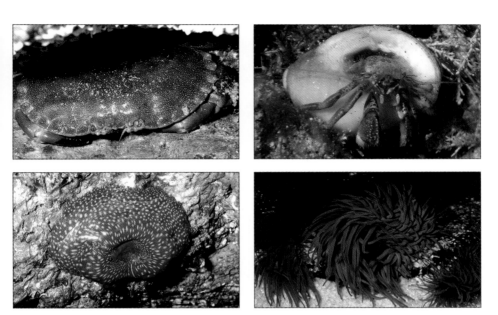

Clockwise from top left: Edible crab, hermit crab, snakelocks and strawberry beadlet anemones

on the rocky shores between Daymer and Polzeath. Beadlets can live quite high up the shore, where they are regularly exposed to the air. To minimize water loss they withdraw their tentacles into their body cavities. Snakelocks cannot do this. So they are confined to rock pools, or else they live low down on the shore.

Snakelocks acquire their amazing, technicoloured tentacles from highly pigmented, single-celled organisms that live inside their bodies. When exposed to sunlight, these plant-like organisms photosynthesize their own food, donating a proportion to their host. In return, the snakelocks provide protection and some of the raw materials required for photosynthesis. When energy from sunlight is too low to make food, snakelocks digest their tenants, and their tentacles lose their brilliance.

Left to right: Rainbow wrack, common limpet, Celtic sea slug on dog whelk egg cases

There are many seaweeds in the rockpools. One is *Cystoseira tamariscifolia*. On a cloudy day or when out of water, it looks like any other olive-brown bushy seaweed. But when the sun shines on it at certain angles and its fronds are under water, it has a brilliant blue-green iridescence, and you can see why its common name is rainbow wrack.

Granite headlands at the mouth of the Camel protect the estuary from the most damaging effects of storm waves. Without them, the soft, sedimentary rocks between Daymer and Polzeath would have been swept away long ago. Among the most interesting sedimentary rocks are the strikingly banded Trebetherick slates.

Two creatures living on the slates are the common limpet (*Patella vulgata*) and the nationally rare Celtic sea slug (*Onchidella celtica*). Both are marine molluscs with a head,

a single large foot, and a radula – a band of tissue in the mouth with small rows of teeth to scrape food from rocks. Limpets have a hard conical shell to protect their soft body tissues; Celtic sea slugs have no shell. When threatened by predators or disturbed by heavy surf, limpets pull their shells down over themselves and clamp tightly on to rocks. Celtic sea slugs have a tough, leathery bodycovering armed with glands that secrete a highly distasteful white, glue-like substance. They avoid heavy surf and other adverse conditions by hiding in tiny rock crevices, only coming out after the rocks have been uncovered by the ebb tide, and then only for a couple of hours or so before low tide. So sometimes you might see hundreds of Celtic sea slugs grazing on the rocks, at other times none.

Banded slates at Trebetherick

Polzeath

After an Atlantic storm, when giant rollers reach the shallow waters just off Polzeath, waves crash cleanly on to the long, sandy shore making it a fabulous place to surf.

Surfing is an exhilarating sport, but it has its dangers. Obvious ones include being knocked off the board or being carried out to sea. These can be minimized by surfing only in designated areas, and by heeding the advice of lifeguards. There is, however, a less obvious potential danger concealed beneath the waves. At low tide, half buried in sand and covered by shallow water, lies the lesser weever (*Echiichthys vipera*) – a fish armed with spines that can inject a potent poison into any unsuspecting victim. Although the chances of stepping on a weever are small, puncture wounds can be agonisingly painful, so if you are paddling at low tide, you would be well advised to wear suitable footwear. If you are stung, you should seek medical assistance.

If you explore the strandline at Polzeath and nearby beaches, you might come across cuttlebones, the egg cases of whelks, and logs carrying stalked goose barnacles (*Lepas anatifera*) thrown on to the beach by storm waves. Also, the Gulf Stream regularly brings in exotic jellyfish, giant bean seeds and other items from more tropical waters. One of the jellyfish sometimes seen at Polzeath in huge numbers is the by-the-wind-sailor (*Velella velella*).

Lesser weever fish – half buried in sand with retracted fin (left); fin raised (right)

Freshly beached, the oval float of *Velella* is a beautiful, deep blue colour with a little elevated crest or sail passing diagonally over it. This is not one animal, but a colony of inseparable individuals that carry out different tasks. Hanging suspended from the centre of the disc is an individual that takes in food. Clustered around this are small reproductive individuals. And around the periphery are feeding individuals, which take the form of long tentacles that trail down into the sea to capture small fry.

Surfer at Polzeath (top).
By-the-wind-sailor (above)

Polzeath to Pentire

With no houses to interrupt the view, the wild splendour of the stretch of coast from New Polzeath to Pentire Point is enjoyed by thousands of visitors each year. In 1936, however, Pentire's unspoilt nature was at risk. The area was divided into building plots and put up for sale. Only after local and national protestors raised enough money to donate the land to the National Trust was it saved from becoming a housing development.

Pentire Point

The desire to construct homes at Pentire is not new. It has attracted settlers since pre-historic times. Evidence for this includes the antiquities, often marked as tumuli on maps, that dot the landscape. One such is a bowl-shaped Bronze Age burial mound in the short grass next to the cliff path leading up to Pentire Point. Unlike modern homeowners, our ancestors probably came to the estuary seeking food, shelter, and an easily defended location, rather than magnificent seascapes and easy access to surfing and sailing.

Gorse at Pentire

For sheer natural beauty, few sights surpass that of high maritime cliffs in full bloom. Plants lining the route from Polzeath to the headland at Pentire include those especially adapted to persistent winds and salt-laden spray. In these conditions, plants find it difficult to absorb water and easy to lose it. To overcome the combined drying effects of wind and salt, many maritime species, such as English stonecrops (*Sedum anglicum*) and sea campions (*Silene maritima*), are low-lying and have rather fleshy little leaves with a waxy surface.

Although not confined to the tops of high cliffs, maritime specialists include sea carrots (*Daucus carota*, ancestors of the garden vegetable), rock samphire (*Crithmum maritimum*) and thrift (*Armeria maritima*).

In August, soldier beetles (*Rhagonycha fulva*) are commonly seen on the heads of the sea carrots, where they spend much of their time coupling. Soldier beetles are so-named because they are slender, and often have bright body colours reminiscent of nineteenth-century regimental uniforms of the British army. This particular species is sometimes called bloodsucker because of its reddish colour. Although it preys on other insects that land on the flower heads, and also feeds on the nectar and pollen of the plant, it is completely harmless to humans.

Alongside maritime species are plants more commonly found further inland. These include harebells (*Campanula rotundifolia*), foxgloves (*Digitalis purpurea*) and tree-mallows (*Lavatera arborea*). Harebells are a Cornish

Clockwise from top left: Sea campion, soldier beetles on sea carrot, harebell, thrift

rarity. This lime-loving plant is able to grow on the rock faces of Pentire because the pillow lava supplies the minerals it needs. Foxgloves are not thought of as coastal plants, but even so they appear to be equally at home on a cliff top as on a roadside verge.

Each year the UK has less and less maritime cliff vegetation. Along the North Cornwall coast it is particularly threatened by house building and encroachment by highly intensive agriculture. In places where cliff tops have been enriched by fertilizers, native wild flowering plants have been crowded out of existence by fast-growing cultivars. Fortunately, low intensity farming is practised on the land owned by the National Trust at Pentire Head. Sheep roam freely on the cliff tops to graze on grasses and shrubs. Without this, the cliff tops would soon be smothered by bracken, gorse, or blackthorn scrub.

Pentire Point

Today Pentire Point is a solid perch from which to view the stunning scenery in and around Padstow Bay. But 300 million years ago, it was under the sea – part of Trevone Basin. Mud and sand, eroded from the Caledonian Mountains to the north, were carried by rivers and streams into the Basin. Over millions of years, the sediment piled up, becoming 6,000 metres thick in places. Under incredible pressure, deep-lying mud and sand were transformed into slate and shale.

Soon after the slate and shale were formed, the area was subjected to violent volcanic eruptions caused by movements of the earth's crust. Large land masses crashed into one another, causing the sediment to buckle and fold. The movements ripped open the sea floor, creating fracture lines along which red-hot liquid lava was forced up from the bowels of the earth. Typically, lava has a temperature of between 700°C and 1,000°C. The type of igneous rock it forms depends on how quickly it cools and hardens.

Lava locked between deep layers of shale and slate cooled very slowly; large rock crystals grew, and it became granite. Lava just beneath the sea-bed cooled much faster. It

Pillow lava

hardened into a dense rock called dolorite, which forms much of Stepper Point, the Rumps and Mouls Island. At Pentireglaze it is known as greenstone, because of its colour.

Lava that came into direct contact with sea-water cooled to form pillow-shaped mounds. Such pillow lava forms the rounded cliffs between Pentire Point and the Rumps. There are several outcrops close to the coastal path, and many stones in the hedges are pillow lava. Close examination reveals small holes from which volcanic gases escaped.

The bare rock at Pentire is a harsh and demanding habitat. Frozen by winter frosts, and sizzling hot in the summer sun, few large organisms can tolerate its extremes. When the headland was formed, lichens were probably the first large organisms to grow on the cooled lava flows.

Golden hair lichen (top). Sunburst lichen (above)

Golden hair lichen (*Teloschistes flavicans*)
Golden hair lichen grows out of the rock as exquisite saffron wisps that form branched 'shrubs' up to 4 cm high. Pentire Head is one of a diminishing number of places in the UK in which it thrives. Sheep-grazing helps to protect it from being smothered by bracken or gorse, and reduces the risk of cliff-top fires.

Sunburst lichen (*Xanthoria parietina*)
Sunburst lichen is a wide-ranging species, found on many hard surfaces, including concrete and the roofs of buildings. It can be seen in its greatest glory on rocky outcrops such as those on the cliffs between Pentire Head and the Rumps. It owes its colour to a pigment called parietin in the walls of the fungal cells that form the outer layer of the lichen. The pigment protects the inner cells from being damaged during periods of intense sunshine. Under the fungal cells, algal cells appear as a distinct green band that harvests light to manufacture sugars.

Lichens have evolved from an alliance between fungal and algal cells. The algal cells photosynthesize food. In return, the fungal cells provide protection against the damaging effects of sun, frost and wind. Lichens are extremely efficient at extracting nutrients from traces in the atmosphere. This makes many species particularly vulnerable to atmospheric pollution. The air around the mouth of the Camel blows mainly off the Atlantic, and is clean enough for some of the most sensitive and rare species, such as golden hair lichen.

Although lichens are among the slowest growing of organisms, they occupy the most inhospitable environments on earth. Their growth and decay help crack open rock and form soils in which mosses, grasses and, eventually, perennial plants can take root.

The Rumps and The Mouls

Seen from Pentire Point, the Rumps headland sticks out into the sea like a fish's tail, joined to the mainland by a narrow neck. Now uninhabited, the Rumps was once the site of a thriving community. Archaeological digs in the 1960s unearthed an Iron Age fort that was probably occupied between the fourth century BC and the first century AD. The fort was elaborately protected by a series of three ramparts and ditches, the remains of which survive as earthworks across the neck. Each rampart led to a defensive gateway that opened on to a flattish area large enough to hold flocks of sheep and several circular wooden huts. Artefacts, including bones and shells, suggest that the fort-dwellers wove cloth from sheep's wool, harvested shellfish from the sea, and cultivated grain. Shards of pottery indicate that they traded as far as the Mediterranean for wine and other luxuries.

Rumps Point is a good place from which to view seabirds on The Mouls. Only a few hundred metres from the Point, the island is far enough away from human activity and most land-based predators to enable puffins and other auks to breed relatively undisturbed.

The Rumps

Razorbills (*Alca torda*), puffins (*Fratercula arctica*) and guillemots (*Uria aalge*) are all members of the auk family: oceanic birds, expert divers and underwater swimmers that spend much of their lives out at sea, but which come inshore to breed. All three species nest on The Mouls, and can often be seen flying close to Pentire Point.

Puffins were once so abundant on The Mouls that it became known locally as Puffin Island. Sadly, in recent years numbers have been in steep decline, partly due to predation and habitat destruction by great black-backed gulls. These large predators not only swallow whole puffin, they also destroy their habitat by tearing up grass during courtship displays. Pollution by chemical wastes and oil have also contributed to the decline. Despite these pressures, a small population of puffins still breeds on the island.

Prior to nesting, puffins come together just offshore to form rafts in which courtship takes place. After courtship, the nesting colony is established on the Island. Eggs are laid from early April – one white egg per clutch in a shallow burrow excavated by the bird itself, or a burrow previously occupied by a Manx shearwater, or rabbit. Hatched puffins are fed by both parents. After being fattened up for about 40 days, the young are abandoned by the parents. Fledglings usually quit the nest at night, taking off from a suitable point, or just flying straight out from the nest to the sea where they fend for themselves.

Fulmar (*Fulmarus glacialis*) is another notable seabird that lives on the high cliffs around Pentire. Because of its plumage pattern, a fulmar is sometimes mistaken for a gull, but it belongs to a different group that includes

The Mouls in heavy seas

Clockwise from top left: Guillemot, razorbill, puffin, fulmar

the petrel, shearwater and albatross. Unlike gulls, all have tubular nostrils. The fulmar's double-tubed nostrils have been linked to the bird's exceptional sense of smell and its ability to assess its own speed when in flight, but their functions are still much debated. If disturbed by a predator or an over-inquisitive birdwatcher, the fulmar projects a jet of evil-smelling oily liquid over the intruder – a sure sign that it wants to be left in peace.

Clumsy on land, fulmars have extraordinary powers of flight. They are extremely agile in the air, twisting and turning with precision close to cliffs, even in strong winds.

If you are on top of Pentire when a north-westerly gale blows towards the shore, you might see an uncommon migrant such as a Cory's shearwater (*Calonectris diomeda*), a Leach's petrel (*Oceanodroma leucorhoa*), or an Arctic skua (*Stercorarius skua*).

Padstow to Stepper Point

Tregirls and Stepper Point from Padstow (above).
Red valerian – Padstow Pride (right)

After returning on the ferry, you can explore the rest of the western side of the estuary by following the well-marked coastal path from Padstow to Stepper Point.

The path is less exposed to the prevailing winds than that on the eastern side of the estuary. In places, the relative shelter allows tall hedgerow plants to grow. Among these are honeysuckle (*Lonicera periclymenum*) – a climbing plant whose long-tubed orange, yellow or purple flowers produce such a sweet-smelling scent. Another is valerian, known locally as Padstow Pride (*Centranthus ruber*).

The dense red, pink or white flower heads of Padstow pride add vibrant colour to many parts of the estuary. As well as lining the deep path to Stepper, they feature strongly along the Camel Trail, in the Slate Quarries and on the embankments leading into Padstow.

The route to Stepper takes you past the sand dunes at Tregirls. Although smaller than those at Rock, the flora and fauna are similar.

One of the most dramatic features of the Camel Estuary is Doom Bar. It lies just off the cliffs south of Stepper, and extends across the estuary to the channel near Trebetherick Point. Lurking just beneath the sea at high tide and with waves crashing over it, this treacherous bank of shifting sand demands great respect from even the most experienced boat-handler. Over the last 200 years it has wrecked hundreds of vessels.

Although its precise boundaries vary with movements of the water channels, at present Doom Bar fills much of Hawker's Cove and Harbour Cove. During a low tide, when the enormity of the sandbank is revealed, you can roam freely over its rippled sand to collect shells and seek other signs of sea life.

Each year, over 100,000 tonnes of sand are dredged from Doom Bar and other parts of the Camel, in an effort to keep the water channels open. But dredgers are fighting

Hawker's Cove from Tregirls Beach

a losing battle: for every tonne of sediment removed, the tides bring in just over a tonne. The dredged sand is not wasted; being rich in calcium, farmers use it to improve soils.

Charlie Watson-Smyth, the tenant farmer and Countryside Steward for Stepper Point, manages the headland in ways that help protect this outstanding part of the Camel and its wildlife. In particular, he is working with the RSPB to conserve corn buntings (*Miliaria calandra*). The UK population of this rather plain brown bird with the 'song' like jangling keys, declined by more than 85 per cent between 1970 and 1998. He hopes to boost numbers by a late harvesting of corn, which will give the birds a chance to breed.

Other farmland birds that will benefit from the conservation measures are skylark (*Alauda arvensis*), linnet (*Carduelis cannabina*)

Left to right: Skylark, linnet, stonechat (male)

and stonechat (*Saxicola torquata*). In recent years the skylark and linnet populations have plummeted in the UK, putting them on the Red List of Birds of Conservation Concern.

There can be few sounds more evocative of a warm summer's day than the liquid warbling of a skylark as it rises vertically into the air and hangs high above the ground. Its song draws you upwards and raises the spirits.

Stonechat is not of conservation concern in the UK, but it is in Europe as a whole, making it an Amber List species. In addition to being common on low bushes around Stepper and Pentire, stonechats frequently perch on gorse on the dunes at Rock and Cant Hill, uttering their distinctive call that sounds like two stones being tapped together. Stonechats also nest and breed at St Enodoc, close to where golfers tee off, seemingly not disturbed by the occasional hook or slice.

The conservation measures of the tenant farmer are supported by the National Coastwatch Station at Stepper Point. As well as their normal duties, station officers keep a watchful eye on wildlife at the mouth of the estuary, and act as a reporting base for sightings. Among the many sightings recorded in 2006 were bottle-nosed dolphins (*Tursiops truncatus*), grey seals (*Halichoerus grypus*), basking sharks (*Cetorhinus maximus*) and gannets (*Sula bassana*). The watch officers were very concerned that some casual weekend boat-owners were harassing the dolphins and basking sharks. Harassments were logged and reported to wildlife agencies.

Basking sharks are gentle giants. Fully-grown, they can weigh some 7 tonnes and grow to 10 metres long. On sunny days, they often cruise just below the surface, and feed on plankton. With their mouths gaping wide, they draw in huge volumes of water

Bottle-nosed dolphin (left). Grey seal (right)

which they filter though a giant sieve made from cartilaginous extensions of the gills.

In summer large numbers of gannets come down to the mouth of the Camel. They create quite a spectacle when, with wings folded back, they dive from a great height into the sea to feed on fish and squid.

If you look towards Newquay from the Coastwatch Station, you can see some of the finest cliffs in the country. Places like Tregudda Gorge and Stack Rock are breeding sites for some of the most common seabirds seen on the Camel. Among these are shags and cormorants. Both are large birds with black, shining plumages. They are sometimes seen together in the mouth of the estuary, bobbing in and out of the water in their search for food. At first glance they are easily confused; the creamy-white markings on the throat of

the cormorants are the only clearly visible distinguishing feature. A detailed study reveals that they are two separate species, with quite distinct ways of making a living.

Cormorants (*Phalacrocorax carbo*) prey mainly on bottom-feeders such as flatfish, prawns and shrimps. They are often more colonial than shags. They tend to nest on small rocky islands and broad cliff ledges that are relatively exposed to the elements. Their nests are up to a metre wide and 80 cm high.

Shags (*Phalacrocorax aristotelis*) feed mainly on surface-swimming prey, especially sand eels and herring. They choose more sheltered coastal sites for breeding, and make their nests in rock crevices, ledges in the roof of caves, or among boulders on steep slopes. Their requirements for space are quite modest; a ledge of 30 cm square is sufficient for

Tregudda Gorge

their nest. Cormorants are common in the upper reaches of the estuary, while shags are a more coastal species.

If you look seaward from Stepper, you will see Gulland and Newland rocks and the vast expanse of the Atlantic beyond. The rocky outcrops mark the official outer limit of the estuary, and the end of our explorations.

From top: Gannet, cormorant, shag